GUINNESS WORLD RECORDS

GUINNESS WORLD RECORDS ™

MYSTERIES & MARVELS OF THE PAST

Historical Records of Phenomenal Discoveries

Collect and Compare with

FEARLESS FEATS:
Incredible Records of Human Achievement

WILD LIVES:
Outrageous Animal & Nature Records

JUST OUTRAGEOUS!:
Extraordinary Records of Unusual Facts & Feats

DEADY DISASTERS:
Catastrophic Records in History

GUINNESS WORLD RECORDS

MYSTERIES & MARVELS OF THE PAST

Historical Records of Phenomenal Discoveries

Compiled by Celeste Lee & Ryan Herndon

For Guinness World Records:
Laura Barrett Plunkett, Craig Glenday,
Stuart Claxton, Michael Whitty, and Laura Jackson

SCHOLASTIC INC.
New York   Toronto   London   Auckland   Sydney
Mexico City   New Delhi   Hong Kong   Buenos Aires

Guinness World Records Limited has a very thorough accreditation system for records verification. However, while every effort is made to ensure accuracy, Guinness World Records Limited cannot be held responsible for any errors contained in this work. Feedback from our readers on any point of accuracy is always welcomed.

© 2006 Guinness World Records Limited, a HIT Entertainment Limited Company.

ISBN-10: 0-439-89827-7
ISBN-13: 978-0-439-89827-0

Designed by Michelle Martinez Design, Inc.
Photo Research by Els Rijper, Sarah Parrish, Alan Gottlieb
Records from the Archives of Guinness World Records

12 11 10 9 8 7 6 5 4 3 2 1   6 7 8 9 10/0

Printed in the U.S.A.

First printing, November 2006

Visit Guinness World Records at www.guinnessworldrecords.com

Contents

A Record-Breaking History

The idea for Guinness World Records grew out of a question. In 1951, Sir Hugh Beaver, the managing director of the Guinness Brewery, wanted to know which was the fastest game bird in Europe — the golden plover or the grouse? Some people argued that it was the grouse. Others claimed it was the plover. A book to settle the debate did not exist until Sir Hugh discovered the knowledgeable twin brothers Norris and Ross McWhirter, who lived in London.

Like their father and grandfather, the McWhirter twins loved information. They were kids when they started clipping interesting facts from newspapers and memorizing important dates in world history. As well as learning the names of every river, mountain range, and nation's capital, they knew the record for pole squatting (196 days in 1954), which language had only one irregular verb (Turkish), and that the grouse — flying at a timed speed of 43.5 miles per hour — is faster than the golden plover at 40.4 miles per hour.

Norris and Ross served in the Royal Navy during World War II, graduated from college, and launched their own fact-finding business called McWhirter Twins, Ltd. They were the perfect people to compile the book of records that Sir Hugh Beaver searched for yet could not find.

The first edition of *The Guinness Book of Records* was published on August 27, 1955, and since then has been published in 37 languages and more than 100 countries. In 2000, the book title changed to *Guinness World Records* and has set an incredible record of its own: Excluding non-copyrighted books such as the Bible and the Koran, *Guinness World Records* is the best-selling book of all time!

Today, the official Keeper of the Records keeps a careful eye on each Guinness World Record, compiling and verifying the greatest the world has to offer — from the fastest and the tallest to the slowest and the smallest, with everything in between.

Where was that found?

For more than 50 years, Guinness World Records has been collecting the facts and stories behind the world's most amazing record-breakers. In this collection, we focus on digging up an answer to the question: "*Where was that found?*"

In search of clues to our civilization's beginnings, historians have unearthed phenomenal discoveries — from the earliest written language to the creation of our most popular organized sports — and proved that one event could transform humankind's future.

Trace the origins of robots back 500 years to an Italian artist. Search for clues among abandoned temples hidden in jungles and deserts. Decipher the messages of giant pictures etched into the ground. These are some of the mysteries and marvels we'll explore inside. Many more secrets of our ancestors are out there, waiting to be discovered!

Chapter 1
Monumental Mysteries

Gigantic circles of stone, cloud-piercing pyramids, and elaborately carved temples challenge us to solve the mysteries beneath these monuments. Who built these structures? How were such massive stones moved into place? What secrets of ancient mankind are stored inside?

Largest Trilithons

The simplest structure is a trilithon: two vertical stones supporting one horizontal stone. The **Largest Trilithons** are at Stonehenge, on the Salisbury Plain, England (pictured). In 2800 BCE, workers ringed this sacred ground with wooden posts. Centuries later, only the largest stones remain. Each of these enormous vertical stones, or megaliths, weighs almost 50 tons — moving one stone required approximately 550 men! Some were carved from a blue-tinted stone fabled for its magical healing properties. It is unknown how these rare stones, found only in present-day Wales, were transported 250 miles to Stonehenge.

The stone circles found throughout the British Isles were built by the Beakers, a Neolithic-era people named after the area's excavated pottery. Stonehenge may have been a temple, a burial ground, or an astronomical calendar. Today, it is a protected site while archaeologists analyze its ancient puzzle.

Around the Henge

Neolithic Britons erected many circles of large stones, known as henges. Avebury is the Largest Ancient Stone Circle, covering 28.4 acres in Wiltshire, UK, with a site date of 4200 BCE. An embankment 30 feet high and a ditch 40 feet wide encircle the henge. Two avenues of stones lead into the circle. The circle itself is made of 100 unquarried stones and is 1,200 feet in diameter. Originally, there were also two inner circles. People didn't realize Avebury was a henge until it was "rediscovered" in 1646. Take a visual tour of Avebury in this book's special color insert.

Largest Obelisk

Carved from single boulders, Egyptian obelisks were a pair of slender sundials guarding temple entrances. The Largest Obelisk is 107 feet 7 inches tall, weighs 502 tons, and can be viewed only in Rome. In 357 CE, Emperor Constantine removed Tuthmosis III's obelisk from Aswan, Egypt. Of the 28 surviving Egyptian obelisks, only 7 remain in Egypt!

The Tallest Obelisk (finished in 1884) stands 555 feet 5 $\frac{1}{8}$ inches high in Washington, D.C. (pictured) An aluminum capstone supported by more than 36,000 stones form the Washington Monument, built in honor of the first president of the United States of America.

Oldest Pyramid

It was an honor to build, and to be buried under, a pyramid. These structures housed royal tombs and ensured a safe life in the hereafter for the pharaohs. The **Oldest Pyramid**, the Djoser Step Pyramid in Saqqara, Egypt (2630 BCE), is a six-level, 204-foot pyramid (pictured). Imhotep was a high priest, astronomer, and the royal architect of the Great Pyramids (see the special color insert). He designed this pyramid in honor of Djoser, the second pharaoh of the Third Dynasty. The royal tomb lies at the bottom of a vertical shaft, 191 feet underground. It was discovered still sealed by a three-ton piece of granite. However, neither Djoser nor Imhotep's mummy was inside! Instead, the pyramid revealed only a mummified foot belonging to an unknown person who died 500 years *after* Djoser's reign.

Largest Pyramid

In terms of actual volume, not height, the **Largest Pyramid** is the Great Pyramid of Cholula de Rivadavia, 63 miles southeast of Mexico City, Mexico. Dedicated to a feathered serpent deity named Quetzalcóatl, this temple stands 177 feet tall, and its base encompasses nearly 45 acres. In comparison, the Great Pyramid at Giza covers 13 acres. Cholula's total volume is estimated a third larger, at 4.3 million cubic yards, making it the **Largest Monument Ever Constructed.** Building started as far back as 800 BCE, with additions from several Mesoamerican civilizations, including the Aztecs. In 1519 CE, Cortez and his invading Spaniards massacred the unarmed local populace. He promised to build the same number of churches as local temples — 365, one for each day of the year — but did not complete his task. The pyramid survived because the Spaniards mistook it for a massive hill and built a church on top (pictured)! Five miles of excavated tunnels give a glimpse into an earlier time with more awaiting discovery.

Largest Ziggurat

Scientists theorize the architectural similarities between ziggurats and pyramids exist because ancient societies traded knowledge of monument construction. Ziggurats were houses for the society's gods, not human beings. Characteristics of this building type are multiple receding tiers, color-glazed bricks, and a summit temple. The **Largest Ziggurat**, built in 1250 BCE by an Elamite named King Untash, is located 18.6 miles from Haft Tepe, Iran. The Ziggurat of Choga Zambil has an outer square base of 344 feet, with three of the original five levels intact (pictured). Choga Zambil was lost to the sands of time for 2,500 years until its discovery in 1935, during an oil company's aerial survey.

Mesopotamia is the land between the Tigris and Euphrates rivers, considered the cradle of civilization. A sophisticated society named the Sumerians traded throughout the Mediterranean and perhaps into India. Ur was their wealthy capital city, located in modern–day Muqayyar, Iraq. This is the site of the Largest Surviving Ziggurat, built by King Ur–Nammu (2111 – 2095 BCE). Time reduced the original three-story structure with a summit temple to two stories at 60 feet high off a base measuring 200 feet by 150 feet. See more phenomenal discoveries made at Ur throughout this book and in the special color section.

Largest Temple

Fishermen near the Tonle Sap Lake in 18th-century Cambodia whispered about temples built by giants until French explorer Henri Mouhot documented finding "the lost city" in 1860. Deciphered inscriptions on the complex's 72 major monuments identified the site as the capital city of a rich Khmer kingdom (880 – 1225 CE), with an estimated population of 80,000 people. The **Largest Temple** is Angkor Wat (City Temple), built under King Suryavarman II's rule (1113 – 1150 CE) for the Hindu god Vishnu. Five beehive- shaped, carved towers crown this three-level monument (pictured), ringed by a 570-foot wide moat. Thousands of bas-relief sculptures and murals depicting Hindu mythology adorn its walls.

In 1431, the neighboring Thai empire ransacked the capital. Abandoned, Angkor Wat lay forgotten until Mouhot's rediscovery. Today, it is an active Buddhist temple. Archaeologists suspect other temples await discovery amid the surrounding 50 miles of jungle.

Out of the Seven Wonders of the Ancient World, the only and oldest surviving wonder is the Great Pyramid at Giza, built by Pharaoh Khufu in 2566 BCE (see the special color insert). Originally 481 feet tall, it is now 451 feet, with 2.3 million blocks averaging 2.5 tons each! Excavations of the workers' living areas estimate 20,000 people built this monument to withstand time.

The Other Six Wonders:

- Hanging Gardens of Babylon — built by Nebuchadnezzar II for his wife (604 – 562 BCE)
- Statue of Zeus at Olympia — Pheidias used gold and ivory at 40 feet high in 440 BCE
- Temple of Diana at Ephesus — 127 columns at 60 feet high by Lydian King Croesus: destroyed by Goths in 262 CE
- Mausoleum of Halicarnassus — built by Queen Artemisia for her husband in 353 BCE
- The Colossus of Rhodes — Chares' 110-foot-high bronze statue of Apollo in 282 BCE
- Lighthouse of Alexandria — started in 290 BCE by Ptolemy Soter; destroyed by earthquakes in 1326 CE

Chapter 2
Pieces of Life

Survival depends upon a group's ability to live and work together. The foundations of society can be traced back to these clusters of the earliest civilizations. We'll sift through the pieces to uncover an extensive burial ritual and the development of simple, important structures such as walls, bridges, and homes.

Oldest Complete Mummy

Societies vary in burial customs. The word *mummy*, derived from the Arabic *mumiya*, means wax and refers to preserving the body. Egyptians believed life after death required six elements: (1) physical body, (2) shadow, (3) name, (4) *ka* (spirit), (5) *ba* (personality), and (6) *akh* (immortality). These beliefs meant proper mummification was an elaborate 70-day process.

All the organs, except the heart, were removed. Fragrances and 600 pounds of natron (salt found near the Nile River) dried the corpse before it was wrapped in 4,000 square feet of linen bandages and sealed with resin, a natural glue. The **Oldest Complete Mummy** is Wati, an Egyptian court musician, of 2400 BCE. His remains were found in 1944, from the tomb of Nefer in Saqqara, Egypt. Pictured is a skull of a Chinchorro mummy, preserved by the sophisticated techniques of mummification and the parched sands of Chile's Atacama Desert.

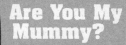

Are You My Mummy?

Many mummies, but not all, have identification amulets wrapped inside their bandages. One mysterious mummy discovered in a small oddity museum in Niagara Falls, New York, turned out to be 3,000-year-old Pharaoh Ramses I (ruled 1293 - 1295 BCE). He had been sold by grave robbers in the 1860s and displayed next to a five-legged pig! The mummification process made DNA testing difficult. Other technological advances, such as digital scans and forensic reconstruction, aided scientists in finally identifying him by comparing skull shapes to royal relatives, such as his descendant pictured on the front cover of this book. Ramses' mummy has since been returned to his Egyptian homeland.

Earliest Habitational Structure

Prehistoric humans took shelter wherever nature provided, such as in caves and beneath rock outcroppings. Gradually, humans shaped and built their own dwellings. The **Oldest Habitation** is the clustered remains of 21 pebble-lined pits and holes for structural wooden stakes (not pictured). Found in October 1965 at the Terra Amata site in Nice, France, these remnants are thought to be wooden huts of the Acheulian culture from 400,000 years ago. Small poles, buttressed by rocks, formed the hut walls. Larger central poles held up a thatched roof. The dwellings were 26 to 50 feet long, 13 to 20 feet wide, and featured an early fireplace. A circle of large and small stones framed by bracing branches made a hearth area where people gathered to cook, eat, and sleep. Terra Amata yielded numerous bones and tools. Analysis of bones and coprolites (fossilized human feces) indicated these people ate seasonal plants and animals extinct today.

Oldest Zoo

The **Oldest Zoo**, located in modern-day Puzurish, Iraq, housed animals collected during war raids in other lands and exotic beasts for religious rituals. Established by King Shulgi, Third Dynasty ruler (2097 – 2094 BCE) of the powerful Sumerian capital city of Ur, this practice was adopted by later monarchs. In the 1600s, King Charles I had a python in his private collection. In 1752 Vienna, the public was granted access to a private collection. In 1847, the London Zoological Society opened its doors. It was the first time people recognized the scientific and cultural purposes of studying animals. Londoners shortened the name, and since then, people worldwide enjoy spending time at the zoo!

The Sumerians prospered after they learned how to manage the rivers bordering them. They created methods to drain flooded lands, purify drinking water, and irrigate crops. By 3000 BCE, the region boasted dozens of highly developed cities from Babylon to Nineveh, radiating from the capital city of Ur, located at the head of the Persian Gulf. This harbor city became the seat of Sumerian society, most likely the largest city in the world (2030 – 1980 BCE). Its population of 65,000 invented ziggurat temples, zoos, writing (75 years before the Egyptians!), math, the wheel, and even board games! Keep digging throughout this book for more historical treasures found at Ur.

Oldest Bridge

People traveled in ancient times despite such obstacles as rivers, valleys, canyons, and gorges. Early on, someone figured out travel would be easier and faster by creating a structure to directly connect two points rather than walking around the obstacle. Apart from placing a wood log across a creek, historians discovered the first bridge was built in — you guessed it — Mesopotamia. The **Oldest Bridge**, which is amazingly still in place, is a single-arch bridge over the river Meles in Izmir, Turkey. The stone bridge has been in use since 850 BCE. Pictured above are the remains of another Turkish stone bridge, where citizens are trying to balance historical preservation with necessary modernization.

Longest Wall

Survival depends upon defense against others. The **Longest Wall** was designed to stop Northern invaders. The Great Wall of China began construction during the Ming Dynasty, at the end of the 14th century, and continued through the beginning of the 17th century. The Mings simply improved upon an existing fortification. The first Emperor of China, Qin Shi Huangdi (221 – 210 BCE), completed the first Great Wall. Various tribes had made different wall structures of packed earth and wood. Qin (pronounced *chin*) ordered these walls to be combined into one long wall with multi-story watchtowers every few miles. Later rulers expanded the Wall. At its longest, the Wall is believed to have been 6,200 miles. Currently, its mainline length is 2,150 miles east to west, varies from 15 feet to 39 feet high, and is 32 feet thick in spite of its fairly poor condition (pictured above and in the special color insert). This defensive structure never fell. The Manchus invaded and conquered China in 1644 because a general opened a gate.

Chapter 3
Art of the Ancients

The desire for self-expression generates music, writing, painting, and sculpture. This spark to create art has burned within humanity since the earliest civilizations. We see the evidence for ourselves. We can handle musical instruments made of bone, read picture stories painted upon cave walls, puzzle over the riddle of lines carved into the ground, and walk a labyrinth.

Tuneful Work

The *shaduf* is a device still in use for lifting water from the Nile River. The ancient Egyptians invented the *shaduf* for watering crops and perhaps for pyramid construction. A long beam is suspended 8 to 10 feet above the ground. A rope connects a bucket hanging on the beam's thinner end and a counter-weight at the opposite end. A worker tugs on the rope and the bucket submerges into the river. When the bucket is full, the worker releases the rope and the beam's counterweight drops, thereby raising the bucket. For thousands of years, irrigation workers at the Nile water mills performed the Oldest Song, a three-note *shaduf* chant, sung in accompaniment to this repetitive task.

Oldest Musical Instrument

Once dinner was ready and a fire built, even the earliest humans wanted entertainment. Scientists speculate our oldest form of expression, music, began 200,000 years ago. The "why" remains a mystery: perhaps a courtship ritual, a hunting lure, or to accompany dancing. We know the "how." A Neanderthal campsite, discovered in 1998 by paleontologist Dr. Ivan Turk in Ljubljana, Slovenia, contained the **Oldest Musical Instrument**. The shape and position of four round holes dug into a bear's femur bone resemble a modern flute. Three holes are in a straight line, with the fourth located in the thumb position. The artifact dates between 43,000 and 82,000 years old. A scientist made a flute using a 50,000-year-old bone — and played it!

Oldest Known Iconic Sculpture

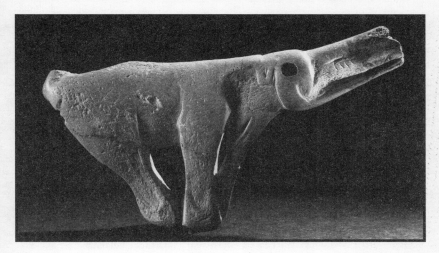

Groups of prehistoric humans did not limit their activities to basic survival. The **Oldest Known Iconic Sculpture** found in Tolbaga, Siberia, is presumed to be a bear's head carved from the vertebra bone of a woolly rhinoceros. The sculpture is more than 35,000 years old! Other figurative sculptures by prehistoric mankind have been found in present-day Europe, including this mammoth carved out of reindeer antler dated 11,000 BCE excavated in France (pictured). A female figurine of a serpentine found in Galgenberg, Austria, dates from 32,000 years ago. Another famous stone sculpture is "Tan-Tan," a 400,000-year-old quartzite figurine found in the sands of Morocco. Scientists debate whether Stone Age man was capable of "artistic" thought or whether the stone is the result of natural weathering. Maybe you will be the one to determine the truth!

Largest Geoglyphs

An enduring mystery lies on the desert ground of Nazca, Peru. The **Largest Geoglyphs** are 300 gigantic figures (geoglyphs) sketched into the soil (pictured here and in the special color insert). The designs occupy 190 square miles and average 600 feet in length, although one arrow exceeds 1,600 feet! Moving surface pebbles to reveal pale pink sand underneath created these soil drawings. The lines, perfectly and eerily straight, travel across furrows and hills. In the 1920s, airplanes flying across the Peruvian pampas reported seeing what appeared to be primitive landing strips. There are drawings of a hummingbird, monkey, spider, lizard, pelican, stylized plants, and unusual geometric figures. South of the geoglyphs, archaeologists located the 2,000-year-old abandoned city of the line-builders, the Cahuachi.

Numerous theories attempt explanation of the Nazca lines. Their enormous size — most can only be appreciated by aerial surveillance — suggests to some imaginative people that the Cahuachi had flying vehicles. Other hypotheses about the purpose of the Nazca lines include an astronomical observatory, a link with the naturally preserved mummies discovered in the area, an astrological calendar, or surface markers for underground water sources in one of the driest places on the planet.

WHEN EXCAVATING MYSTERIES . . .

© Ed Collacott/Photographer's Choice/Getty Images

GLORY OF THE GREAT
Once there stood Seven Wonders of the World. Today, the Great Pyramid at Giza (center) erected by Pharaoh Khufu is the oldest and sole surviving wonder. Wander through more massive structures in "Monumental Mysteries."

OR DOCUMENTING MARVELS

© William A. Allard/National Geographic

BLURRING THE LINES
Scientists search for an explanation beneath the unexplained pictures engraved into the ground at Nazca, Peru. Nature and mankind are gradually erasing the lines' beauty. View more stunning visuals carved around the world in "Art of the Ancients."

THESE PHENOMENAL DISCOVERIES

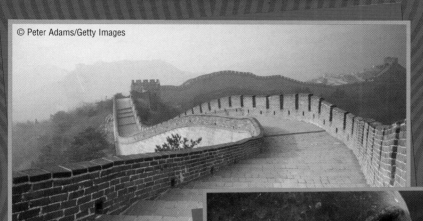

© Peter Adams/Getty Images

WITHSTOOD TIME

© O. Louis Mazzatenta/National Geographic/Getty Images

BUILT TO LAST
The First Emperor of China, Qin Shi Huangdi, made a lasting impact on Chinese culture by building the Longest Wall and the Largest Tomb. Investigate the awesome power behind the thrones with "Royal Leaders."

FASCINATED ARCHAEOLOGISTS

© Sandro Vannini/CORBIS

CIRCLES OF LIFE

Henges are sacred areas of large stones arranged in circles. The most famous is Britain's Stonehenge, but Avebury is the Largest Stone Circle. Sort through "Pieces of Life" to learn more about how our ancestors lived.

REVOLUTIONIZED THOUGHT

© iStockphoto

© Robert Harding/Digital Vision/Getty Images

SHOW AND TELL

Cave paintings demonstrated our ancestors' artistic development. Egyptian hieroglyphics shared much of their culture. But ancient people's deepest secrets were passed along verbally. Decipher clues from lost civilizations in "Signs & Symbols."

INTRIGUED EXPLORERS

© Stuart Westmorland/CORBIS

LOOK OUT BELOW

Underwater archaeology explores sunken mysteries, from recent shipwrecks to seagoing vessels lost centuries ago. These lost wrecks shed light upon a culture's trading practices. See what was bought and sold among "Foundations of Society" and modes of transportation in "Moving Forward."

DELIGHTED GENERATIONS

© Chryssa Panousiadou/epa/CORBIS

ATHENS 2004

© Palais Didier/SuperStock

PLAYING GAMES
Chess is a game for the brain, and the Olympics are competitive games for the world. Many of today's pleasant pastimes originated from war games thousands of years ago. Historic entertainment awaits you in "Games on the Board" and "Games on the Road."

GUINNESS WORLD RECORDS ™

CHANGED OUR LIVES

© Archivo Iconografico, S.A./CORBIS

© Bettmann/CORBIS

FORWARD THINKER
Meet artist and inventor Leonardo da Vinci in "Revolutionary Inventions." See how his mechanical dreams became real machines and continue to influence modern-day inventions in "Moving Forward." Bill Gates, founder of Microsoft, says of da Vinci, "His writings demonstrate that creativity drives discovery, and that art and science — often seen as opposites — can in fact inform and influence each other."

. . . TO BE A GUINNESS WORLD RECORD-HOLDER

Oldest Paintings

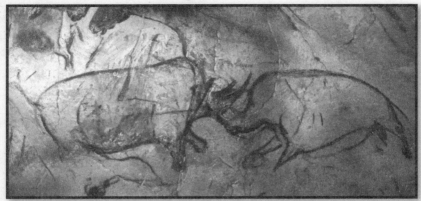

The **Oldest Paintings** are not hanging in a museum. It is on permanent display on the Chauvet cave walls in southwestern France, near Avignon (pictured). Discovered in 1994, the caves were named after one of the spelunkers (a cave explorer). Inside, the cave paintings date between 23,000 and 32,000 years old. Rhinoceros, lions, mammoths, horses, bison, bears, reindeer, aurochs (like cattle, but now extinct), ibex (wild goats), stags (male deer), and owls appear in red and black paint upon the cavern walls. Most of the images are animals, but there are images of human hands cast in negative, and a woman's portrait was identified in 2001. The discovery completely challenged scientific thought, which had theorized that human artistic capability had slowly progressed from primitive scratchings to sophisticated, lively renderings. The Chauvet painters made use of shadowing, perspective, and lines, thus turning our ideas on the origins of art upside down!

Oldest Surviving Hedge Maze

To "walk the labyrinth" is a method of meditation used by people throughout the ages. The classical labyrinth — a single path spiraling through seven rings into a central end point — comes from ancient Greece. However, most labyrinths are free of the Minotaur and built for hours of mind-tricking entertainment. No one yet knows the symbol's meaning or why the pattern repeats in sites throughout Syria, Spain, Italy, India, Peru, the southwestern United States, and the UK. The **Oldest Surviving Hedge Maze** was constructed as an elaborate puzzle, dizzying its wanderers with a total path length of 0.5 miles to its center (pictured). Royal gardeners George London and Henry Wise designed the 0.5-acre maze located at Hampton Court Palace in Surrey, UK, for King William III and Mary II of England. Planting began in 1690, with other gardeners and several trees repairing and replacing the original set throughout the centuries.

Chapter 4
Signs & Symbols

How would we learn about history and its people if events were not recorded? Although early Egyptian hieroglyphs and Sumerian cuneiform tablets were discovered, these crucial documents were still mysterious signs until we found the keys to deciphering these ancient symbols. Before we start tracing the history of our own language, do you know which letter of the alphabet is the oldest?

Earliest Alphabet

The alphabet took centuries to "grow up." The Sumerians used pictographs to represent words in 3500 BCE. They wrote in vertical columns, pressing a reed into clay. When a topic couldn't fit onto one tablet, a "book" of tablets was bound together by leather. People realized horizontal writing was faster, and used a wedge-tipped reed called a stylus to simplify pictographs into cuneiform symbols (pictured). No one could read cuneiform until 1835, when British army officer Henry Rawlinson found inscriptions in three languages — Old Persian, Babylonian, and Elamite — on a cliff in Behistun, Persia. The Behistun inscription translated cuneiforms, with its deciphering equivalent for hieroglyphics found in the Rosetta stone.

The **Earliest Alphabet** we know about was found in the early 1990s — and dates back to 1900 BCE! Yale University Egyptologist John Darnell found symbols representing sounds carved into limestone in Wadi el Hol, near Luxor, Egypt.

Oldest Letter

From A to Z

The Phoenician alphabet had 20 letters, including the **Oldest Letter** still in use. The letter "O" has never changed shape since its first use around 1300 BCE. In addition to trading goods throughout the Mediterranean, the Phoenicians brought their alphabet to the Greeks, who changed some of the shapes for their purposes. The word *alphabet* comes from the first two letters of the Greek alphabet — Alpha and Beta. In Italy, a variation of the Greek alphabet became the mother of the Etruscan alphabet, around 500 BCE. The Etruscans changed many of the letters' shapes and added a letter (upsilon, U). The Romans adapted Etruscan writing, added X, Y, and Z, and swung B in the direction it's used now. Our modern letters are direct descendants of Roman letters (Latin).

The original Roman (or Latin) alphabet had 21 letters:

**A B C D E F Z H I K L
M N O P Q R S T V X**

Around 250 BCE, Z was dropped because there was no specific sound to go with it, but G was added. Later, Y and Z were added, but at the time were just used for Greek words. W was introduced in the 7th century CE as a double V by writers of Old English, and made it into common usage by 1300. The **Newest Letters** added to the English language are J and V. J used to be a variation of I, and V was a variation of U. By 1630, these letters were established consonants and vowels.

Earliest Surviving Personal Name

Do you know what your name means? Some people think their personal name influences the person they become. That's why some parents study the origins and meaning of a name before choosing it for their child. The **Earliest Surviving Personal Name** we know of belonged to a pre-dynastic king of Upper Egypt, who ruled before the Age of Pharaohs in 3050 BCE. His personal name is shown as an early hieroglyph of a scorpion (pictured). It is suggested the name should be read as "Sekhen." Graffiti from that time said that "King Scorpion" won a battle. At times, his scorpion hieroglyph is shown with a falcon hieroglyph — apparently the falcon meant that he was the king! Try to decipher more hieroglyphics shown in the special color insert of this book.

Earliest Written Language

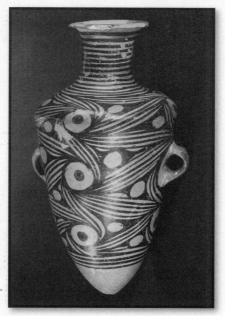

Another hot spot for early civilization was prehistoric China. People of the Yangshao culture, which thrived in present-day Shaanxi province, built reed-hut houses, polished stone tools, and crafted red and black earthenware pottery (pictured). Alongside these developments, the Yangshao conceived the idea of writing. The **Earliest Written Language** can be seen on pottery from Paa-t'o, which shows early characters of the numbers 5, 7, and 8. This evidence of mankind's first step from an oral to a written culture was simplistic — primarily vertical and Z-shaped lines. Found in 1962 near Xi'an, the pottery dates between 5000 and 4000 BCE.

Earliest Autograph

The excavation of Ur was as archaeologically important as Howard Carter's 1922 discovery of King Tut's tomb. Pioneering archaeologist Sir Charles Leonard Woolley, Director of the University of Pennsylvania Museum, led a joint excavation of Ur's royal tombs from 1922 to 1934, funded by the Pennsylvania and British Museums (pictured). Among the great treasures unearthed were numerous cuneiform clay tablets. Since then, 500,000 tablets have been discovered. The writings unite the puzzle pieces of lost civilizations, from pottery shards to mummified musicians, and share the stories of these people's lives. Their doctors and medicines, goods traded, religious and scientific beliefs, farming and irrigation techniques, politics and war. Only skilled scribes possessed the rare and powerful knowledge of writing. The **Earliest Autograph** is from such a scribe named A-Du who added *dub-sar* after his name, which translates as "Adu, scribe." Found in Tell Abu SalAbikh, Iraq, the tablet dates from 2600 BCE!

Scribe Star

Making papyrus was another ancient Egyptian secret never written down and kept for the exclusive use of the royalty. Egyptian papyrus, an early form of paper made from a plant found along the Nile, has as much to reveal as clay tablets. The Leningrad Museum, USSR, displays a papyrus by the scribe Ameni-amen-aa dating from 2130 BCE, that tells the story of a shipwreck survivor who washes up on an island ruled by a talking serpent! The **Earliest Surviving Signature** is found at the end: "This is finished from its beginning unto its end, even as it was found in a writing. It is written by the scribe of cunning fingers, Ameni-amen-aa; may he live in life, wealth, and health!"

Chapter 5
Foundations of Society

People are always hungry for knowledge. There were even universities during the earliest societies. Telling time and regulating crop irrigation became critical skills to grow more food and feed more people. Active trading of goods led to the invention of money. Here, we look closer at what makes society tick.

Oldest Coin

Ancient trading was a barter system. For example, 1,000 sheaves of wheat for one goat. Other commodities used as "money" were salt, conch shells, gold ingots, and large stones. In pre-revolutionary America, wampum, maize, iron nails, tobacco, and beaver pelts were preferred methods of payment.

The Kingdom of Lydia, flourishing 1000 – 546 BCE in present-day Turkey, minted its own money during the reign of King Gyges. These renowned merchants may have used the metal discs as money, religious offerings, or treaty payments. The **Oldest Coin** was made of electrum, a gold and silver alloy found in local rivers. By 630 BCE, Lydian coins, or trites, were marked with the king's emblem, a roaring lion's head (pictured). What was a trite worth? One expert said 11 sheep, another 10 goats, and another 3 jars of wine!

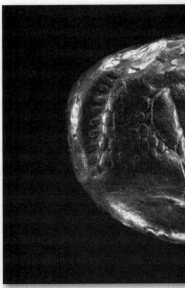

Pricey Prophecies

The phrase "rich as Croesus" refers to the last King of Lydia, Croesus, who was exceptionally wealthy (see illustration). Because Lydia had plenty of electrum, Croesus literally minted money. By his reign, Lydians had also mastered making all gold and silver coins. King Croesus is said to have offered many coins to the mysterious Oracle at Delphi (in Greece) for prophetic advice in warring against the Persians. The Oracle predicted that if Croesus crossed the river, he would destroy a great kingdom. Croesus did start a war, but the Lydians lost, and their great kingdom of Lydia was the one destroyed.

Largest Waterwheel

Waterwheels were the forerunner to today's hydroelectric dams. A waterwheel is a simple machine that harnesses the power of water. As flowing water turns a wheel, buckets positioned on the outer rim lift water up and out to aqueducts or irrigation canals. Numerous waterwheels on the Orontes River helped create a prosperous agricultural society as early as Roman times. Hamath, an old city mentioned in the Bible, now called Hamah in present-day Syria, is the home of the Mohammadieh Noria waterwheel. Its wheel is 131 feet in diameter — that's 10 stories high! You can still see the **Largest Waterwheel** in action alongside an original Roman aqueduct (pictured).

Oldest Observatory

An observatory is a place for astronomers and stargazers to watch the skies for planetary changes. The reverse occurred when NASA spotted the **Oldest Observatory** of Abu Simbel in Egypt (pictured). Carved between 1284 – 1264 BCE during the reign of Pharaoh Rameses II, these two temples were originally constructed to emphasize the culture's belief that their pharaoh was a sun god. The larger temple measures 108 feet high and has four statues (of Rameses, and deities Ra-Horakhty, Ptah, and Amun) in its sanctuary. On two special days, the king's birthday (February 20) and coronation day (October 20), the shining sun would bask all four statues. However, the installation of the Aswan High Dam (1964 – 1968) required relocation of the temples for flood prevention. Since then, the sun's crowning event occurs one day later.

Oldest Hotel

Humans traveled far to find food and shelter. Naturally, people began searching for ways to move faster than walking and looked for places to stay instead of the nearest cave.

According to legend, the god of Hakusan Mountain in Japan told a Buddhist monk about a secret underground hot spring in a nearby area. The hot spring turned out to be the real deal, and the priest's disciple, named Garyo Hoshi, built a *ryokan* (hotel) and spa on the site. The Hoshi Ryokan at the village of Awazu, Japan, became famous for its miraculous healing powers and has been in the same family since 717 CE (pictured). The **Oldest Hotel** is currently run by the 46th generation of Hoshis, and guests eager to take a dip in the wonderful waters fill the inn's 100 bedrooms.

Oldest University

Learning is crucial for the advancement of civilization. Students gather to hear experts verbally share their knowledge. The Sumerians founded the **Oldest University** in 3500 BCE. This school for scribes, called *É–Dub-ba*, translates into "tablet house." It was highly competitive and expensive to attend a scribe school. Rich and influential families aided their ambitious Babylonian and Akkadian sons striving for schooling. The first step in securing a good job in government or at the temple was to learn vocabulary and practice good handwriting. Scribes also learned law, business, record keeping, literature, letter writing, mathematics, surveying, and music. All are courses taught in today's schools worldwide. The **Oldest Existing Educational Institution** in the world is the University of Karueein, founded in 859 CE. Located in Fez, Morocco, Karueein is still considered an important center of learning.

Chapter 6
Royal Leaders

The fascination with powerful people is nothing new to any society. People have always been interested in those wielding control over their lives. Let's flip through the pages of history to meet kings with the shortest and longest reigns, a small survivor of a violent revolution, and an imperial family whose grip on the throne is still unchallenged.

Oldest Royal Family

Today, many countries enjoy democracy, a system of government where citizens vote for their leadership. In ancient days, rulers such as pharaohs, kings, queens, emperors, and czars seized their thrones by divine right, claiming the gods chose them or they were a type of god.

The **Oldest Royal Family** or Ruling House is the imperial family of Japan, who are directly descended from Emperor Jimmu (660 – 581 BCE). He claimed to be an earthly descendant of the sun god, Amaterasu. (Many historians believe Jimmu ruled later, around 40 BCE.) After World War II, the emperor became a symbolic figurehead. An elected prime minister and cabinet governed Japan. An enormous reverence for royal history remains. The current Emperor Akihito ascended in 1989 as the 125th ruler of the Chrysanthemum Throne. His son, the Crown Prince, has no male heirs. Although there have been empresses in Japan's past, current Imperial law forbids a female ruler, and the populace is concerned about the country's royal future (pictured).

Longest All-Time Reign

Shortest Reign

Many pharaoh mummies are missing, including the record-holder for **Longest All-Time Reign**. A Sixth Dynasty Pharaoh of the Old Kingdom, Pepi II ascended the throne at age six with his mother as co-regent (pictured). When of age, he assumed sole rule for 94 years, (some Egyptologists dispute this figure). During his era, governmental power shifted dramatically to regional rulers. The building of his funerary complex near the Djoser Step Pyramid was unaffected. While not as grand as the Great Pyramids of the Fourth Dynasty, he and his several wives each commanded substantial monuments. Historians theorize Pepi II's obsession with the afterlife drained his pharaonic power over the people.

The House of Bragança came to rule Portugal in 1640. A split from Spain, a government exodus to Brazil, a devastating earthquake, fatal disease, revolutions, and much intrigue ensued. The royal family of Bragança also holds the record for **Shortest Reign** of any ruler ever. Crown Prince Felipe and his father the king were shot on February 1, 1908. His father died immediately, and Felipe technically became King of Portugal, Dom Luis III, for about 20 minutes. His younger brother Manuel succeeded him.

Largest Single Tomb

In early China, whenever Shang Dynasty kings died, their property was buried with them — this included wives, servants, bodyguards, horses, and dogs. This burial custom ended during the Zhou Dynasty, yet the society continued preparing its rulers for the afterlife in rituals similar to Egyptian customs.

In 1974, farmers near Xian uncovered the tomb of Emperor Qin Shi Huangdi, builder of the original Great Wall (see Record 10). He also employed a horde of 700,000 laborers to create the **Largest Single Tomb**, a 20-square mile underground palace known as the Mount Li tomb. Its massive dimensions were 7,129 by 3,195 feet, and 2,247 by 1,896 feet, respectively. Emperor Qin ascended when he was 13 (221 – 210 BCE). Obsessed with gaining immortality, Qin studied alchemy and died while in search of the Islands of Immortality, supposedly located east of China. His death was kept secret for fear of governmental collapse. Tremendous speculation exists about what lies beneath his tomb. The royal treasury may have been buried with him. We know what is inside four tomb vaults: more than 7,000 life-size terracotta soldiers and horses. Each statue is exquisitely formed, complete with individual facial expressions and hairstyles, in full battle dress — an eternal army for Qin's afterlife (pictured on the right and in the special color insert).

Greatest Kidnapping Ransom

The legendary golden city of El Dorado lured Spanish conquistadors for two centuries. El Dorado's location remains a mystery, but its story mesmerized treasure-seekers of the New World. In 1524, conquistador Francisco Pizarro, cousin of Hernan Cortés who conquered Mexico (see Record 3), sought the Inca civilization. After several failed expeditions, Pizarro returned to Spain to seek royal permission for a final expedition. He arrived in Cajamarca, Peru, in 1532, where his small force of 200 shot thousands of unarmed Incas and captured Atahualpa, the Emperor (see illustration). Atahualpa knew the Spaniards desired gold and offered a colossal ransom for his release: one room filled with gold and two more rooms of silver. It took two months, but the Incas brought 16 tons of gold, worth at least $1.5 billion, to pay the **Greatest Kidnapping Ransom**. However, Pizarro had no intention of keeping his word. He staged a mock trial and executed Atahualpa. This tragedy marked the demise of the Inca Empire.

Greatest Number of Royals Killed in a Revolution

The hope of finding a "common" person descended from royal blood became an obsession after 1919. The Russian people, suppressed by the old feudal system, violently revolted against the ruling Czar. The Bolsheviks captured Czar Nicholas II, Czarina Alexandra, their five children, and seven other relatives in Yekaterinburg, Russia. The **Greatest Number of Royals Killed in a Revolution** equaled 15 members of the Romanoff family. Rumors flew about the youngest children, Anastasia and Alexei, eluding death. In the 1990s, following the fall of Russian communism, the secret burial site of the Romanoffs was revealed. Anastasia's remains were found, but not Alexei or Maria, the older sister!

Playing Princess

The Anastasia mystery fascinates the world. Several people claimed to be of the Romanoff line, but Anna Andersen was the most famous royal hopeful. Discovered in 1922 Berlin, Anna had a striking physical resemblance and an advanced education typical of Russian royalty. In 1964, she died in Charlottesville, Virginia, believing she truly was Anastasia. But in 1994, DNA testing proved definitively that she was not a Romanoff (pictured).

Chapter 7
Games on the Board

What's *your* favorite board game? People love playing chess, checkers, and dominoes. Did you know that these games have been around for thousands of years? Someone had to invent the games and their rules. Let's roll the dice for a glimpse at the origins of our most enduring board games.

Oldest Chess Pieces

Playing the game of chess is believed to be a mark of high intellect. Several countries — India, China, Greece, Ireland, Egypt, Assyria, and Arabia — lay claim to its origins. The earliest written reference comes from ancient Persia. The battle game of *shah* (meaning ruler or king) is cited in the *Chatrang Namak*, dated 6th century CE. Chess was a war game, called *chaturanga*, using four army divisions — each part inspired its own chess piece: infantry (pawn), chariots (castle), cavalry (knight), and elephants (which became the bishop in elephant-less Europe). The phrase "checkmate" likely comes from *shāh māt* meaning "the king is finished" in Persian. Evidence is rare because archaeologists find it hard to distinguish between decorative sculptural figurines and actual game pieces. Researchers feel confident the **Oldest Chess Pieces** specifically made for game-playing date to 900 CE and come from Nashipur, in present-day Bangladesh. Visit the special color insert for more game play.

Earliest Book About Checkers

What game did Abraham Lincoln, Thomas Edison, Harry Houdini, and the people of Ur all enjoy? Checkers! An early version of the game board found in Ur had a different design and number of pieces. In Egypt, a 5 x 5 square version of the checker game board was a popular pastime by 1400 BCE. By 1100 CE, a Frenchman had the bright idea of placing backgammon men on a chessboard that moved in a similar fashion to the popular game of the time, *alquerque*. Jumping pieces became mandatory for a clear winner. In 1547, Antonio Torquemada, of Valencia, Spain, penned the **Earliest Book About Checkers**. His rules were similar in form to how we play the game today, with 12 "men" on each side of an 8 x 8 game board (although a 10 x 10 board is globally familiar). Pictured above is the Hawaiian version played with black and white stones on a grooved stone surface.

Largest Electronic Darts Tournament

The idea of darts came from practicing archery. Some experts say that the invention of the bow and arrow was as important as learning how to make fire. They enabled man to catch food more easily and defend himself from larger predators. Archers became leading warriors because their skills were crucial in both successful offense and defense. Archery practice in smaller spaces using wine barrel bottoms or tree trunks as the target inspired the game of darts. The modern game's board scoring was invented in 1896 by Brian Gamlin (UK). Today, darts are evolving with technology. The **Largest Electronic Darts Tournament** held in Barcelona, Spain, on March 26 – 28, 2004, saw 5,099 individual players competing for bulls-eyes. Electronic darts are soft-tipped with an electronic-activated scoring board versus the classic steel-tipped darts and natural sisal board (pictured).

Jigsaw Puzzle with the Most Pieces

Like many hobbies and sports, jigsaw puzzles started out with more serious intentions. In the 1760s, an English mapmaker named John Spilsbury pasted maps onto wood and cut them into smaller pieces using an agile saw named a jigsaw. These "dissected maps" were an educational tool for children to learn geography. In the 1900s, the wealthy bought hand-carved game boards with non-interlocking pieces and without any idea of the final, assembled picture. Industrialization brought cardboard backing and mechanized "jigsaws" for faster mass production and cheaper prices. Puzzles exploded in popularity for all ages. Just like Spilsbury, today's puzzlemakers construct geography puzzles using detailed maps (pictured). The Youth Committee of the Singapore History Museum completed the **Jigsaw Puzzle with the Most Pieces** on June 29, 2002. It had 212,323 pieces, and the end result measured 35 feet 5 inches by 38 feet 3 inches.

Most Dominoes Toppled by a Group

In 1922, archaeologist Howard Carter discovered the tomb of Tutankhamen, the boy pharaoh nicknamed King Tut. His intact tomb contained multiple treasures, including a solid-gold funerary mask (see sidebar) and an ancient set of dominoes.

These tiles with dots or pips represent numbers and are used for several games: block games, using all tiles; point games, accumulating high tile values; and match games, creating tile sets. The most popular game is toppling one tile after another (pictured). The record for **Most Dominoes Toppled by a Group** was set at FEC EXPO in Leeuwarden, Netherlands, on Domino Day (November 18, 2005). The amount of tiles toppled that day was 4,002,136! This beat the previous 2002 record involving 3,847,295 dominoes falling in 51 interlinked displays, including a 16.5-foot pyramid that King Tut might have enjoyed building.

Toppling Tut

The boy king's reign began at age 9 in 1334 BCE, and ended at age 19. His mysterious death haunted historians. Many thought the young pharaoh was murdered, because initial X-rays showed a hole in the back of his skull. In 2005, advanced digital scans proved King Tut died of a terrible infection from a broken leg. The resulting embalming and mummification process caused the suspicious hole in the skull.

Chapter 8
Games on the Road

Everybody likes a *good sport*. But did you know that "being a good sport" is as important now as it was thousands of years ago? Our journeys will take us to: Greece, where honoring Zeus led to recognizing excellence in mortal athletes; Scandinavia, where chasing reindeer resulted in one of our most popular winter sports; and Mexico, where bouncing balls in the New World transformed into basketball!

Earliest Accurately Dated Olympic Games

The Olympics' esteemed reputation stems from its ancient heritage and global participation. The **Earliest Accurately Dated Olympic Games** occurred in July 776 BCE. Existing records declare Coroibos won the one *stade* (200 feet) foot race. The footrace was the sole event for the first 13 Olympics! Archaeological evidence shows that festivities took place for hundreds of years before this date. These religious celebrations included sacrifice, poetry readings, a trade fair, and feasting. Individual athletes shed shoes and clothing during competitions. The winner received an *athlon*, an olive wreath crown (no silver or bronze), and competed for their home state's glory.

The Greeks devised the pentathlon — one event with a discus throw, javelin throw, long jump, footrace, and wrestling match. The **Oldest Surviving Olympic Measurements** date from 656 BCE: Chionis of Sparta won the long jump at 23 feet 1.6 inches; Protesilaus won the discus at a 100 cubit throw (about 152 feet). The original Olympics lasted until 396 CE, when Roman Emperor Theodosius declared it a pagan festival and abolished it. The modern Olympic Games debuted in the summer of 1896, fittingly held in Athens, Greece. This illustration depicts the marathon won by Spiridon "Spiros" Louis. Today's Athens Olympic Stadium is also named after him.

Marathon Man

Legend speaks of Phidippides, a soldier who ran 24 miles from Marathon to Athens, Greece, in 490 BCE. He died after delivering news of the Greek victory over the invading Persians. His effort is immortalized in the running of the marathon. At the first modern Olympics in 1896, Greek shepherd Spiridon "Spiros" Louis ran the race in 2 hours 58 minutes and 50 seconds (pictured). The official marathon length of 26.5 miles became fixed with the Oldest Marathon, run in Boston every year since 1897. Today, there are all types of marathons, including skipping, baby-carriage pushing, and three-legged races!

Earliest Evidence of Organized Running

Activities once critical for hunter-gatherers evolved into sports for enjoyment among settled communities. Running, jumping, and throwing became the premise of competition at celebrations like the Olympics (pictured in the special color insert). The purpose was to act out myths of important deities, or gods. Funeral rituals in those days included sporting competitions (see illustration). According to Homer's *Iliad*, the warrior Achilles held funeral games in honor of Patroclus, his fallen friend. But the Greeks don't win the record race! The **Earliest Evidence of Organized Running** dates back to 3800 BCE in Memphis, Egypt. Ritual races were run around city walls, overseen by the pharaoh who was considered a god in Egyptian society.

Most Ancient Ski in Existence

Skiing was crucial to successful hunting in Neolithic Scandinavia, and reindeer provided food, clothing, and tools for early humans (see illustration). Found in a peat bog in Hoting, Sweden, the **Most Ancient Ski in Existence** dates from 2500 BCE. It measures 44 inches long, 3.75 to 4.1 inches wide, with a hollowed-out footrest, and a hole for primitive binding. The oldest skis were carved from animal bone.

Rock carvings of skiers found in Russia date from 6000 BCE. Skis, like bows and arrows, became a skill set during wartime. The **Earliest Recorded Military Use of Skiing** was at the Battle of Isen, near Oslo, Norway in 1200 CE. King Sverre of Norway ordered local civilians to spy on enemy positions. Later in 1296 CE, a loyal countryman transported the infant Norwegian prince Hakon Hakonsson to safety by ski. This journey is repeated annually in a 34-mile race from Lillehammer to Rena with 6,000 skiers carrying an eight-pound backpack to represent the baby.

Highest Scoring Average in NBA Season

Ball playing has mythic origins. The Olmec in Mexico played ball on a court in present-day Paso de la Amada, Mexico, around 1000 BCE. The name *Olmec* means "rubber people," and their game carried complex religious significance. Mayans and Aztecs enjoyed the game, with even Conquistador Cortez taking ball players back to Spain. In the Aztec *Ollamalitzli* game, the player won all the spectators' clothing if the solid rubber ball went through a fixed stone ring!

Luckily for us, the rules changed in December 1891. That's when Dr. James Naismith, YMCA athletic director in Springfield, Massachusetts, devised an indoor game of 13 rules, two peach baskets, and a soccer ball. Instantly popular, the game of basketball entered Olympic competition in 1936. The record-holder of **Highest Scoring Average in NBA Season** for any basketball player is Wilt Chamberlain (pictured). He scored an average of 50.4 points per game during the Philadelphia Warriors' 1961 – 62 season.

Largest Prize for a Single Horse Race

Around 6000 BCE, humans domesticated horses. By 2000 BCE, trained equine pairs towed chariots in Mesopotamia. A horse was the ultimate war weapon. Tribes with horses grew larger, more powerful, and richer because owning horses was expensive. In ancient Egypt, one horse ate 10 acres of barley each year.

Racing horses in sport developed swiftly. The *Iliad* talks about chariot races in Troy in 13th century BCE. By 648 BCE, chariot racing was a main event at the XXXIII ancient Olympiad. In 210 CE, the Roman Emperor Lucius Septimius Severus (146 – 211 CE) organized the **Earliest Horse Race** among imported Arabian steeds in Netherby, Cumbria, UK. A speedy horse can win you more than an *athlon*. The **Largest Prize for a Single Horse Race** is a purse of $6 million awarded at the annual Dubai World Cup (pictured). The race is held in the United Arab Emirates and the winner gets $3.6 million!

Chapter 9
Moving Forward

Can you imagine a world without cars, boats, trains, and planes? It makes you wonder how early humans managed to get from one place to another . . . especially across deserts and oceans. Becoming mobile with a set of wheels, an engine, and wings was definitely the way to go. Take a look at the evolution of transportation as we chart the high seas, get on land with two- and four-wheel devices, and lift off into the skies!

Earliest Surviving Vessel

Some of our most history-changing artifacts are found in peat bogs throughout the UK, Scandinavia, Germany, and the Netherlands. While building a highway in 1955, the **Earliest Surviving Vessel**, a well-preserved prehistoric pinewood canoe, was found in a small bog near Pesse, Netherlands. It was mistaken for a tree trunk and left on the roadside, where a farmer later saw it and realized that it was a boat! The dugout is almost 10 feet long, and has been carbon dated between 6315 and 275 BCE. It is now on display in the Provincial Museum in Assen, Netherlands. Bogs also preserve people amazingly well. Found in the same area, Yde girl is a 16-year-old bog mummy (pictured). Scientists can determine her hair, eye and skin color, age, and overall health. Such finds have been the subject of intense investigation. Was the girl murdered or did she die by accident? Only time and more research will tell if a crime was committed centuries ago.

Oldest Shipwreck

The seafaring life is a key aspect of Mediterranean societies. A shipwreck meant that everything was forever lost to the sea. Until 50 years ago, when the use of compressed air in deep-sea diving made underwater archaeology possible for amateur and professional divers worldwide. More than 1,000 Mediterranean wrecks have already been identified, yet no warships have been found. The **Oldest Shipwreck** known to date is off Uluburun, near Kas in southern Turkey. The vessel's remains are from the 14th century BCE. The Institute of Nautical Archaeology's excavation lasted from 1984 to 1994. The ship lay on a steep slope at a depth of almost 170 feet. Its cargos, scattered 200 feet down, is one of the wealthiest and largest collections of Late Bronze Age items found at the bottom of the sea. Dive into the special color insert for more underwater treasures.

Plunging into History

Underwater robots, sonar, and positioning technologies are fueling deep-sea exploration. The Black Sea near Turkey yields ancient shipwrecks because the sea floor is without oxygen and bottom-dwelling sea creatures. Entire wooden ships and intact food have survived thousands of years. This odd process of mummification for ships resulted in the **Deepest Shipwreck** found so far using side-scanning sonar on November 28, 1996. The *SS Rio Grande* was a World War II German runner sunk by the Americans in 1944. The ship lies 18,904 feet down in the South Atlantic Ocean — three times deeper than the *Titanic*!

Earliest Bicycle

An invention is a new object or process created through imagination and/or ingenuity. They are often improvements upon earlier ideas. The **Earliest Bicycle** is an example of a milestone where many contributed to the end result. A device with wheels, foot pedals, and cranks, invented by Scottish blacksmith Kirkpatrick MacMillan in the 1840s, was declared to be the first bicycle (see illustration). An 1817 *draisine* by Baron von Drais was a bike in concept, but you had to push your feet against the ground to move along. MacMillan's pedal bike didn't catch on, but the French-developed *velocipede* in the 1850s with huge front wheels did. The bigger the wheel, the faster the pace — especially because 99% of the energy you put into pedaling is transmitted to the bike wheels. Innovation continued rapidly, and the chain-driven Rover safety bike created by James Starley in 1885 is much like today's bike, although air-filled tires didn't make the scene until 1888!

Earliest Automobile

When is a car a car? The word automobile means "moves by itself," stemming from *autos*, Greek for "self," and *mobilis*, Latin for "move." American Henry Ford, maker of the famous Model T and founder of The Ford Motor Company, called his first car a "quadricycle," or having four wheels. History defines the **Earliest Automobile** as the vehicle built by Frenchman Nicolas-Joseph Cugnot in October 1769 (see illustration). Cugnot, a military engineer for the French Army, wanted to make a machine capable of towing heavy cannons. His *fardier á vapeur*, or "steam wagon," could travel at 2.5 miles per hour and haul 4 tons. Cugnot's big idea was to figure out how to convert the energy made from the back-and-forth motion of a steam piston into the rotary motion of the wheels. Two years later, he built a faster one — too fast, because it crashed into a wall, thus causing the world's first car accident.

Earliest Helicopter Flight

Back in 400 BCE, Chinese children enjoyed a toy with a flying top. Barter and trade brought the ingenious toy into Europe. Then this cute toy landed in a 1463 painting. In 1493, Italian artist-scientist Leonardo da Vinci made the **Earliest Helicopter Design** for carrying people into the sky! Discovered in the 19th century, his sketches depicted four people pushing a bar around a central shaft, causing the corkscrew-like shaft to turn and create lift into the air (pictured in the special color insert). His observations about flight were revolutionary and inspired other inventors. Numerous models and test runs later, the **Earliest Helicopter Flight** soared with the French Breguet-Dorand Laboratory Gyroplane in 1935. This was the first helicopter to be fully controllable and fly successfully. In 1942, Igor Sikorsky produced a single-rotor vehicle perfect for mass production of an aerial fleet. Today, many different types of helicopter models whirl through the skies (pictured).

The famous paintings *Mona Lisa* and *The Last Supper* are by Leonardo da Vinci — a genius who symbolizes the interest in science, art, and learning of the Renaissance Age. After the fall of the Roman Empire, Europe fell into a centuries-long decline. Advances of earlier civilizations such as the Mesopotamians, Egyptians, Greeks, and Romans virtually vanished. Leonardo's prolific inventiveness was written into private notebooks, now called codexes. A few of Leonardo's ideas brought to life centuries later include: solar power, vegetarianism, calculators, parachutes, tanks, submarines, underwater diving devices, water turbines, canals, swing bridges, street-lighting systems, and contact lenses! See more of da Vinci's work in the special color insert.

Chapter 10
Revolutionary Inventions

Curious and inventive people have pushed civilization to the advances we enjoy and improve upon every day. Plenty of imagination goes into dreaming up devices, such as a machine to count time, a box that captures pictures, or a mechanical man! Maybe you will invent a machine capable of revolutionizing the world.

Earliest Mechanical Clock

What makes a clock tick? The mechanism is called an escapement. The escapement consists of a two-pronged device that moves back and forth and, as it does, taps the clock's main gear, making a tick-tock, tick-tock sound (pictured). A Buddhist monk named Y. Xing (pronounced *shing*) and a royal engineer named Liang Lingzan invented the **Earliest Mechanical Clock** with an escapement in China. Completed for the Emperor's palace in 725 CE, the clock had a bell-and-drum audio feature that announced the time of the day. It also had a celestial globe surrounded by moving rings, mimicking the sun and moon's actual oribital paths. It was the escapement, however, that dramatically improved the original water clock's accuracy to within 15 minutes a day!

Keep On Ticking

The mechanical clock in England's Salisbury Cathedral started ticking in 1386. It kept time for 498 years, striking only upon the hour, until it was replaced in 1884 by a modern clock. Rediscovered in 1929, the unusual faceless clock was on display until being restored to its original working condition in 1956 (pictured). Today, the Oldest Working Clock ticks along and strikes the hours just as it did in medieval England.

Oldest Dated Cannon

Not all inventions help humanity. Gunpowder was accidentally invented in China during the 9th century. In the 1100s, a military engineer realized that gunpowder could be packed with a ball into a tube sealed on one end. By lighting the gunpowder, the resulting explosion forced the ball out of the tube's open end! In China, balls fired out of bamboo tubes were seen as a great weapon against thick fortress walls. The idea caught on fast and the cannon was considered the most advanced military weapon of its time. Even Leonardo da Vinci designed cannons for the Duke of Milan.

The next challenge was to make a metal cannon that could better sustain the internal explosion. The **Oldest Dated Cannon** is the Dardanelles Gun, cast by the Ottoman Empire in 1464, at the request of Sultan Mehmet II. It was made of bronze, an alloy of copper and tin. The weapon weighs 37,000 pounds and measures 17 feet long. It had a range of 5,249 feet when firing a 670-pound cannonball. The date is engraved on the cannon, which is displayed at the Royal Armouries, Fort Nelson, Hampshire, UK (pictured).

Oldest Known Surviving Photograph

With modern digital cameras, we can snap and see photos in seconds! The idea of capturing images took decades to perfect. Louis Daguerre developed the daguerreotype photograph, but a scientist-inventor named Joseph Niépce (1765 – 1833) produced the **Oldest Known Surviving Photograph** capable of recording images that didn't vanish. This breakthrough happened in 1822 after earlier attempts by others failed to capture the image, or it faded away. The earliest surviving Niépce photograph during this period of intense experimentation is named *View From His Window at La Gras* (pictured). Lost for decades, it was rediscovered in February 1952 by photo historian Helmut Gernsheim after six years of research. The landscape on glass was found in a luggage trunk in London. Today, it can be viewed at the University of Texas in Austin, Texas. Another Niépce photograph of a copper engraving of Pope Pius VII taken at Gras, near Chalon-sur-Saône, France, did not survive the ravages of time.

Earliest Motion Pictures

The Mystery of the Missing Moviemaker

Attaching photographs onto metal won fame for a French photographer-chemist named Louis Aimé Augustin Le Prince (pictured). His experiments led to the 1885 filming of the **Earliest Motion Pictures** in New York City. However, these dim outlines of moving objects faded away. In October 1888, Le Prince patented a single-lens camera that "captured" motion. The *Roundhay Garden Scene* of exposed paper negatives is the **Earliest Surviving Film**. Set in his father-in-law's British garden, this film captured 10 to 12 frames per second. Since paper negatives proved unreliable, he experimented with a sturdier material called celluloid — still in use today.

As the inventor of cinema, why isn't Louis Aimé Augustin Le Prince more famous? The answer is an unsolved mystery. In 1890, Le Prince planned a promotional tour to unveil his patented camera in the U.S. Before his tour, he vacationed with friends in France. On September 16, 1890, his friends saw him board a train in Dijon for Paris. He was never seen again! Not until 2003, when a picture from 1890 of an unidentified drowned man was found in the Paris police archives. The drowning victim resembled the moviemaker. Accident? Murder? The truth disappeared with Le Prince.

Fastest Running Humanoid Robot

Centuries after his death, Leonardo da Vinci's futuristic ideas continue to change our lives. The Japan-based carmaker Honda developed a humanoid robot series in 2000 that isn't too different conceptually from da Vinci's blueprints for a mechanical man. Honda's latest in its series of prototype humanoid robots runs at 1.8 mph, even in circles. (Scientists define "running" as having both feet off the ground at the same time.) Getting ASIMO (Advanced Step in Innovative Mobility) up to speed took years of research in ensuring the robot's steps don't slip or slide.

The current ASIMO is 4 feet 4 inches tall and weighs 119 pounds. The robot's built-in visual, ultrasonic, and floor-surface sensors aids it in pushing carts, avoiding obstacles, and going up and down stairs (pictured). ASIMO's ability to receive and carry objects is achieved through coordinating eye cameras in its head and kinesthetic sensors in its wrists. In November 2004, ASIMO was inducted into the Robot Hall of Fame. Someday, maybe you'll have a robot in your home, doing your chores for you!

BE A Record-Breaker!

Message from the Keeper of the Records: Record-breakers are the ultimate in one way or another — the youngest, the oldest, the tallest, the smallest. So how do you get to be a record-breaker? Follow these important steps:

1. Before you attempt your record, check with us to make sure your record is suitable and safe. Get your parents' permission. Next, contact one of our officials by using the record application form at *www.guinnessworldrecords.com.*

2. Tell us about your idea. Give us as much information as you can, including what the record is, when you want to attempt it, where you'll be doing it, and other relevant information.

> **a)** We will tell you if a record already exists, what safety guidelines you must follow during your attempt to break that record, and what evidence we need as proof that you completed your attempt.

b) If your idea is a brand-new record nobody has set yet, we need to make sure it meets our requirements. If it does, then we'll write official rules and safety guidelines specific to that record idea and make sure all attempts are made in the same way.

3. Whether it is a new or existing record, we will send you the guidelines for your selected record. Once you receive these, you can make your attempt at any time. You do not need a Guinness World Record official at your attempt. But you do need to gather evidence. Find out more about the kind of evidence we need to see by visiting our website.

4. Think you've already set or broken a record? Put all of your evidence as specified by the guidelines in an envelope and mail it to us at Guinness World Records.

5. Our officials will investigate your claim fully — a process that can take a few weeks, depending on the number of claims we've received and how complex your record is.

6. If you're successful, you will receive an official certificate that says you are now a Guinness World Record-holder!

Need more info? Check out the Kids' Zone on *www. guinnessworldrecords.com* for lots more hints and tips and some top record ideas that you can try at home or at school. Good luck!

Photo Credits

The publisher would like to thank the following for their
kind permission to use their photographs in this book: